Git and Gitnub Guide

The Basics

Jerry N. P.

Copyright©2017 Jerry N. P.
All Rights Reserved

Copyright © 2017 by Jerry N. P.

All rights reserved. No part of this publication may be reproduced, distributed, or transmitted in any form or by any means, including photocopying, recording, or other electronic or mechanical methods, without the prior written permission of the author, except in the case of brief quotations embodied in critical reviews and certain other noncommercial uses permitted by copyright law.

Table of Contents

Introduction	5
Chapter 1- Getting Started	6
Chapter 2- GitHub Basics	20
Chapter 3- Setting up SSH Authentication	35
Chapter 4- Social Coding	44
Chapter 5- Hosting Static Websites	52
Chapter 6- Making Code Citable	56
Chapter 7- Managing Repository Collaborators	60
Conclusion	68

Disclaimer

While all attempts have been made to verify the information provided in this book, the author does assume any responsibility for errors, omissions, or contrary interpretations of the subject matter contained within. The information provided in this book is for educational and entertainment purposes only. The reader is responsible for his or her own actions and the author does not accept any responsibilities for any liabilities or damages, real or perceived, resulting from the use of this information.

The trademarks that are used are without any consent, and the publication of the trademark is without permission or backing by the trademark owner. All trademarks and brands within this book are for clarifying purposes only and are the owned by the owners themselves, not affiliated with this document.

Introduction

Many projects are development by a team of individuals rather than by a single individual. If it is a software project for example, there needs to be a proper way of version control. This will help ensure that an individual's update to the project is not overwritten by another user. Git and GitHub can help you achieve this. The Git can only be used via the command line. GitHub provides you with a graphical user interface to use Git. This way, it becomes easy for members of a repository to collaborate towards completing their project. This book guides you on how to use Git and GitHub. Enjoy reading!

Chapter 1- Getting Started

GitHub is a social network that has greatly changed the way we work. It started as a collaborative platform for developers, but it is now the largest online storage space for collaborative works of the world. When you become a member of GitHub, you can use it in the same way you use Facebook and Google. Before GitHub, most companies kept their knowledge in private. However, today you can visit their GitHub accounts and study, download and build upon anything that they have added to their network. The GitHub platform is highly used for hosting social codes. You will find everything on the platform including simple, playful experiments and even the Linux kernel.

Git is the software running at the heart of GitHub. Git is software for version control, which means that it manages any changes made to software without overwriting any part of the project. Suppose you are working with another individual to update the pages of a website.

Once you have made your changes, you save then upload them to the website. A problem will arise when both you and the coworker are working on the same page simultaneously. There are high chances for one to overwrite the works of the other.

A tool such as Git can help you avoid this. The two of you will be allowed to upload their work on the same page, and the tool will save two copies. You can then merge your work together at a later time without losing any details. It is also possible for you to revert back to an earlier version since the Git software keeps a snapshot for each change that is made.

However, the Git software has a problem in that for us to interact with it; we use a command line, or the terminal for the case of Mac users. This means that we have to type snippets of code in order to access it. This can be a tough task for modern computer users who are used to the graphical user interface (GUI) rather than running commands on the terminal and command line.

GitHub helps us overcome this problem. GitHub makes it easy for us to use Git in two ways. First, after downloading the GitHUb software to your computer, you will get a visual interface that will help you control the version as well as your local projects. Secondly, after creating an account at GitHub.com, your version-controlled projects will be available on the web and social network features will be tied for a good measure.

You will be altered to browse through the projects of the other GitHub users, download, alter and use them for learning purposes. Other GitHub users will also be able to do the same to your public projects, and identify bugs and suggest for fixes. Note that no data will be lost since Git saves snapshots of the changes. It is possible for one to use GitHub without having learnt Git.

Installing Git

Before you can begin to use Git, you must first install it.

There are two ways on how you can get Git on your computer. You can install an existing package for the platform you are using or install it from source.

Installing from Source

The advantage of installing Git from source is that you will get its latest version. Each Git version comes with some UI enhancements. Most Linux distributions also have old packages, hence it will be good for you to install Git from source and get the latest version.

Git depends on the following libraries, so ensure you have installed them: curl, openssl, expat, zlib and libiconv. The following commands can help you install the libraries. Choose one of the commands depending on whether your distribution has yum or apt-get:

**apt-get install libcurl4-gnutls-dev libexpat1-dev gettext **

libz-dev libssl-dev

**yum install curl-devel expat-devel gettext-devel **

openssl-devel zlib-devel perl-devel asciidoc xmlto

After you have installed the dependencies, you can grab the latest version of Git from Git website:

http://git-scm.com/download

You can then compile and install it by running the following commands:

tar -zxf git-2.15.1.tar.gz
cd git-2.15.1
make prefix=/usr/local all
sudo make prefix=/usr/local install

Note that you must change the above command (first two) depending on the version of Git that you have downloaded. After that, get the Git via the Git itself for updates:

**git clone
git://git.kernel.org/pub/scm/git/git.git**

Installation on Linux

If you need to install Git on Linux through a binary installer, then use the package management tool provided by the Linux distribution that you are using. If you are using Fedora, use the yum package as follows:

yum install git

If you are using Ubuntu or any other Debian-based distribution, run the following command:

apt-get install git

Installation on Mac

The installation of Git on Mac can be done in any of three ways.

You can get the Git installer and it will provide you with onscreen instructions while installing the Git. Download it from the following link:

http://sourceforge.net/projects/git-osx-installer/

You can also install it via MacPorts (**http://www.macports.org**). If you have already installed MacPorts, you can install Git by running the following command:

sudo port install git +svn +doc +bash_completion +gitweb

There is no need for you to add all the extras, but it wills well for you to add +svn if you need to use Git with subversion repositories. You can also install Git via Homebrew (**http://brew.sh/**). If you have installed homebrew, run the following command in order to install Git:

brew install git

Installation on Windows

It is very easy for you to install Git on Windows. You only have to download the installer, which is an exe file then run it:

http://msysgit.github.io

After the installation, you will have both the command line and the GUI version of Git.

Creating a Local Git Repository

For you to create a new project using Git on your local machine, you should begin by creating a new repository, commonly referred to as a "repo".

Open the terminal then use the cd (change directory) command to move to where you need to place the project. If you need to add the project to a folder on your desktop by the name "GitProject", then you can navigate as follows:

cd ~/Desktop
mkdir gitproject
cd gitproject/

Note we have used the mkdir(make directory) command to create the folder on the desktop. You can then use the "git init" command in order to initialize a git repository at the folder's root. This is demonstrated below:

git init

Adding a New File

We can now add some new file to the project. You can use the "touch" command or any text editor. This is shown below:

touch file.txt
ls

The ls (list) command will display the file since we have created it with the touch command.

Git will notice that changes have been made to the repo and it will keep track of your file. You can run the "git status" command to check the files that are currently known by the git:

git status

The git will notify you that you should use the "git add" command in order to add the file to what is being committed. If you don't run the command, the git will not be able to do anything to the file.

The Staging Environment

In Git, a commit refers to the record of all the files that you have changed since the last time that a commit was made. Essentially, once you have made a change to the repo (such as modifying a file or adding a new one), you must tell git to add the changes to a commit. Commits are very important in git as they will help you to revert to any project state at any time that you need.

The question is, how can you tell the git the files that you need to put into a commit? This is done by the help of a *staging environment*. It is also referred to as the "index". After making a change to a file, git will notice it but it will do nothing to the file.

For a file to be added to a commit, it should first be added to the staging environment. This is done by use of the following command:

git add <filename>

After using the "git add" command to add all the files that you need to the staging environment, you can tell the git to add them to a commit. This can be done by running the "git commit" command.

Once you have added the file to the staging environment via the "git add" command, you can check whether this was successful by running the "git status" command.

Creating a Commit

Now that the file is in the staging environment, it can be committed from there. The commit can be done by running the command given below:

git commit -m "Your commit message"

The message about the commit should be related to what you are committing.

Creating a New Branch

Sometimes, you may be in need of adding a new feature, but you may fear adding it to the main project as you develop the feature. The git branches will help you in such a situation. The purpose of branches in git is to allow you move back and forth between project states.

Suppose you need to create a new page for a website. It is possible for you to create a branch for that page only without any effect on the main project.

Once the development of the page is completed, you can merge the changes in the branch to the master branch. Once a new branch has been created, Git is capable of knowing and tracking the commit that the branch "branched" off of, meaning that it has the history of all the files behind it.

Suppose you are currently on master branch, but you need to create a new branch for development of the page. You should run the following command:

git checkout –b <branch name>

The command will create a new branch and "check you out" on it, which means that the git will move you from the master branch to the new branch.

You can then run the following command in order to confirm whether your new branch was created:

git branch

The branch name that has an asterisk next to it will be the branch that you are currently pointing at currently.

Once you change back to the master branch then you perform a number of commits, the new branch will not see the changes until the time you merge the changes onto the new branch.

Chapter 2- GitHub Basics

Creating a New Repository on GitHub

The repository is a place for your projects to live. It is simply a digital storage space or directory from where you are able to access your projects, the files for the project and all versions of files saved by Git. If you only need to track your code locally, there is no need for you to use GitHub. However, sometimes you may need to work as a team collaboratively in order to modify the code for a project. You should use GitHub.

We need to demonstrate how to create a new repository on GitHub. Login to your GitHub account and go to the home page. You will see a new green button written "+ New repository". GitHub will then ask you to give the repo a name as well as a brief description.

Once you have provided the information, just click the button written "Create repository" and the repo will be created.

You will be asked whether you need to create a new repository from scratch or whether you need to add a repo that you have created locally. Remember we had created a repo on our local computer, so we need to push it to GitHub. This can be achieved by running the following commands:

git remote add origin

https://github.com/nicohsam/gitproject.git

git push -u origin master

Note that you should change the URL in the first command given above to the one listed on GitHub since your username and repository must be different.

Pushing a Branch to GitHub

Our goal is to now push the commit in the branch into the new GitHub repo.

This way, other people will be able to see the changes that we have made. If the repository owner accepts the changes, they will be merged with the master branch.

For you to push the changes onto some new branch on GutHub, you should run the following command:

git push origin yourbranchname

After running the above command, the GitHub will create the branch automatically on the remote repository. In my case, I run the following command to push a branch named "mybranch":

git push origin mybranch

You may be asking yourself the meaning of the word "origin" in the command. After cloning a remote repository into your local machine, git automatically creates an alias for you. In most cases, the alias is known as "origin".

It is simply shorthand for your remote repository's URL. For you to push the changes to a remote repository, you could have used any of these two commands:

git push git@github.com:git/git.git yourbranchname

git push origin yourbranchname

Note that if this is your first time to use GitHub, then you might be prompted to enter your username and password. If you refresh your GitHub page, you will identify a new note saying that a branch that bears your name has been pushed to the repository. You may also go ahead and click the link for "branches" and you will see that the branch has been listed there.

Now, click the green button written 'Compare & pull request". We need to make a pull request.

Creating a Pull Request

A pull request (PR) is simply a way of telling the owner of the repository that you need to make changes to their code. This will make them review their code and ensure that it is okay before they can merge your changes to the master branch.

Once you click the big green button written "Merge pull request", it means that you will merge the changes into the master branch.

However, the button will not be green all the time. Sometimes, you will see it appear in grey color, which is an indication that you are in a merge conflict. This occurs when there is a change in one file which conflicts with what is contained in another file and git is unable to tell the version to use. In such an occurrence, you must get in and tell git the version to use.

Sometimes, you can be a sole owner or a co-owner of a repo, and you may need to create a PR in order to merger your changes. It is always good for you to make a PR so that you may be able to keep history of your changes and ensure that you always create a new branch anytime you need to make changes.

Merging a PR

Just click the green button written "Merge pull request" in order to merge the changes into the master branch. Once you are done, just delete your branch as many branches may mess you. Click "Delete branch" button to delete it.

To verify whether the commits were merged, just click the "Commits" link that can be found on the first page of the new repo. The page will show you all the commits in the branch. Move to the right hand side and see the hash code for the commit. A hash code is simply a unique identifier for a commit. It helps you when you need to refer to a particular commit and when you need to undo changes.

The following command can help you to backtrack or undo a change:

git revert <hash code number>

Getting Changes to the Computer from GitHub

At this point, you have done a lot to the repo on gt he GitHub, making it look different compared to the repo you have on your local machine. Example, you have made a commit on your branch and merged it with your master branch. However, this is not available in the master branch of your local machine. For you to get the recent changes that others or even you have merged on GitHub, you should use the following command:

git pull origin master

After running the command, you will also see all the files that have happened and the way they have changed.

For you to see all the new commits, just run the following command:

git log

Sometimes, you may be in need of switching the branches back to master branch. This can be done using the following command:

git checkout master

Congratulations for making a PR request and merging your code to master branch.

Deleting and Restoring Files

It is possible for you to delete the contents of a particular repository as well as the repository itself on GitHub. Before doing this, it is good for you to check and ensure that you have committed the work to your local repository.

You can use the "git status" command to check for any uncommitted changes or untracked files. Secondly, ensure that all the commits have been pushed to a remote repository.

Checking the Status of the Repositories

For you to review and know the status of both the local and remote repository, it is recommended that you check the last commit in history. For you to be guaranteed that you are aware of all the changes that have occurred in a remote repository, you should run the "git fetch" command before you can review the history. The command will return the state of the remote repository as at the current and any local changes will to be affected. After that, just show the message of the last commit by running the following command:

git log -1

Notice that we have used the parameter -1, which limits the output to our last commit.

The remote repository is normally aliased as "origin", and we can inspect it by running the following command:

git log -1 origin

However, the command given above may fail. If this happens, then specify a branch name to go with remote name. For example, you can try the following:

git log -1 origin/master

The above command means that we have a branch named "master" on a remote repository named "origin". In case the commits differ from each other, you should push the local commits to a remote repository before you can continue.

Once you have verified that everything has been synchronized and that no files are currently left untracked, it is time for you to delete the repository.

The deletion involves the removal of the entire folder which has the ".git/" folder and other details. This is shown below:

$ cd ~
$ rm -rf gitrepository

Note that we have used the remove (rm) command in order to delete the repository with the name "gitrepository".

Restoring the Repository

You may be worried after deleting everything from your repository. However, you don't have to worry since there is a way for you to restore everything and undo what had been done. For you to be able to restore a repository, you should first know the address of your remote repository. This address will be shown at the top of all repository listing. You are also allowed to make a choice between SSH, HTTP and Git Read-only.

The best way to transfer this is via SSH (Secure Shell). Just copy the address then run the commands given below from your home directory:

cd

git clone git@github.com:nicohsam/gitrepository.git .

The command will create a new repository by the name "gitrepository", then copy the ".git/" folder and checkout all the files for you. You can run the following command to check what is in the folder that has been created newly:

ls -1a gitrepository

You will find that all the files and folders have been returned.

Deleting Repository files

In Git, all files under a particular repository are tracked under version control.

It is possible for you to delete all the files and folders that are contained in your current working directory. First, check whether you have committed all the changes by running the "git status" command in the current working directory.

In case you find that you have modified or untracked files, it will be good for you to take care of them before you can proceed.

On GitHub, there are a couple of ways through which you can delete files and folders. You can do it via the file explorer, which will provide you with a graphical user interface on which you can choose the files to delete, and then delete them. You can also achieve this via the command line. When deleting files and folders, take care not to delete the ".git/" folder. The fact that it starts with a dot (.) shows that it is a hidden file. We want to delete all the files that are contained in the "gitrepository" folder. The following commands can help us navigate to the repository and do the deletion:

cd ~/gitrepository

rm -rf **/*

When asked to confirm the deletion, type "y" for yes and the deletion will happen. You can then run the list (ls) command to check the contents of the directory and know what has happened:

ls –la

You will find that only the hidden files like the ".git/" folder will be left. You will then have deleted all the work done on the project successfully. Sometimes after deletes the files for a project, you may need to restore them. This can be achieved by running only a single command. Here is the command:

git checkout .

Don't forget the dot (.) after checkout as it denotes the current directory. Note that the command will not give out any output, so it is your duty to check whether the restoration was successful or not. Just run the "ls -1a" command and all contents of the directory will be listed.

Chapter 3- Setting up SSH Authentication

You can use SSH (Secure Shell) to connect to GitHub. When using the SSH protocol, you are able to connect and authenticate to remote services and servers. If you have the SSH keys, you will be able to connect to GitHub without the need for you to provide your username and password each time you visit GitHub.

Checking the Existing SSH Keys

Before you can generate any SSH key, it is possible for you to check whether you have any SSH keys. To do this, open the Git Bash then run the following command on it:

ls -al ~/.ssh

Check the listing of the directory to see whether you have any public SSH key.

By default, filenames for public keys should be one of the following:

- id_dsa.pub
- id_ecdsa.pub
- id_ed25519.pub
- id_rsa.pub

In case you have no existing public and private key pair, or in any case you don't wish to use any of the available keys, then you can go ahead and generate another one. If you see a listed public and private key pair and you would like to use it for establishing a connection to GitHub, then you can add the SSH key to ssh-agent.

How to Generate a New SSH Key

If you need to create a new SSH key that you will use to connect to GitHub, you should generate then add it to ssh-agent. If you don't have an SSH key, then it is a must for you to generate one.

After adding the key to the SSH agent, you will not have to enter the passphrase. The SSH agent is responsible for management of SSH keys and it will remember the passphrase.

To generate the SSH key, follow the steps given below:

1. Open the Git Bash then paste the following text on it. Ensure that you substitute the email contained in the text with your email address:

   ssh-keygen -t rsa -b 4096 -C
   email@example.com

   The command will create an SHH key and the email you provide will be used as a label.

2. When you see the prompt for "Enter a file in which to save the key," just hit the enter key. It will accept the default location of the file.

3. On the prompt, just type a secure passphrase once prompted to do so, then confirm by reentering it.

Adding SSK Key to SSH-Agent

Now that you have checked for the existing keys and generated an SSH key, you can add your new SSH key to the ssh-agent for management. In case you have installed the GitHub Desktop, it is possible for you to use it for cloning repositories instead of dealing with SSH keys. The tool comes with Git Bash tool, which is the best way for you to run the git commands on the Windows operating system.

Follow the steps given below|;

1. Ensure that the SSH agent is running.

    For those using the Git shell that comes installed with the Git desktop, ssh-agent should be up and running. If you are using some other terminal prompt, then you should do something in order to auto-launch the ssh-agent.

The SSH agent will be launched automatically once you open the Git shell or the bash. To do this, open the ~/.profile or ~/.bashrc file in the Git shell then paste the following lines of code in them:

env=~/.ssh/agent.env

agent_load_env () { test -f "$env" && . "$env" >| /dev/null ; }

agent_start () {
   (umask 077; ssh-agent >| "$env")
   . "$env" >| /dev/null ; }

agent_load_env

 # agent_run_state: 0=agent running w/ key; 1=agent w/o key; 2= agent not running

agent_run_state=$(ssh-add -l >| /dev/null 2>&1; echo $?)

if [! "$SSH_AUTH_SOCK"] || [$agent_run_state = 2]; then

```
    agent_start
    ssh-add
elif [ "$SSH_AUTH_SOCK" ] && [ $agent_run_state = 1 ]; then
    ssh-add
fi

unset env
```

The assumption is that the private key has been stored in the default location, which can be ~/.ssh/id_rsa or ~/.ssh/id_dsa. If this is not the case, then you must tell the SSH authentication agent where you have stored the private key. To add the key to ssh agent, type the following:

ssh-add ~/path/to/my_key

Once you run bash of it's your first time, you will be asked for a passphrase. Just type it. The ssh-agent process will run until the time you shut down your computer, log out or kill the process.

Other than starting the ssh-agent manually, it is possible for you to start it manually and run it in the background. The following command will help you do this:

eval $(ssh-agent –s)

Note that the $ is part of the command but not the prompt, so type the whole of the command as written above.

2. Now, you can add the ssh private key to ssh-agent. If you used a different name when adding the key, or if you need to add an existing key with a different name, the *id_rsa* should be replaced with the name of the private key file in the command given below:

ssh-add ~/.ssh/id_rsa

GitHub should then be configured so that it can use the existing SSH or a new one that you have generated.

This calls for the addition of the key to the account. To do this, follow the steps given below:

1. First, copy your SSH key to the clipboard.
   If the SSH key file bears a different name to the one in the command given below, then change the filename in order to match the setup that we have currently. When copying the key, avoid adding whitespaces or newlines.

   clip < ~/.ssh/id_rsa.pub

   The command will copy the contents of the file named id_rsa.pub to the clipboard.

2. On any page, move to the upper right corner, clic your profile photo then click on Settings.

3. In the sidebar for user settings, click "SSH and GPG keys."

4. Next, click either "Add SSH key" or "New SSH key".

5. Type a descriptive label for the key on the "Title" field.

6. Copy the paste your key in the field for "Key".

7. Next, click "Add SSH key" in order to add the key.

8. You may be prompted to enter your GitHub password, so just do so.

Chapter 4- Social Coding

Coding on your own can be boring. You should note that GitHub is not place to host code only, but it is a platform that makes collaboration easy.

There are two ways through which one can contribute to the repositories of others.

First, you can add a user as a collaborator to your own project. This will grant the user a full access to your project. They will be in a position to commit any changes directly into your repository. This becomes of importance if you trust the user very well and you are sure that they cannot mess with your project. If you can't trust the user, then don't do it.

Forking

On GitHub, forking is the process of creating an exact of someone's repository then putting it into your account. After that, you will be in a position to make any changes that you need as it is your code.

Note that after forking someone's repository, they will be notified of the same. When they try to view the copied repo on your account, they will be able to see that it was "forked from" them, and everyone will be able to see the inventor of the code. For you to fork a GitHub project, you just have to click the "Fork" button located next to it. After that, wait for the forking to complete. Once done, you will be taken to the copy of your forked project.

Keeping the Fork Synced

You might have formed a project for the purpose of proposing changes to the upstream, or the original repository. In such a case, you should keep your forked project synced with the upstream repository. For you to implement this, you should use Git on the command line.

Creating a Local Clone of a Fork

You have managed to fork a project, but the files for

the repository are not currently available on the local computer. Let us now create a clone of the fork on our local computer:

1. On your GitHub account, navigate to the fork that you have created.

2. Under the name of the repository, click "Clone or download".

3. In the section for Clone with HTTPs, copy the clone URL for your repository by clicking the button pointing to the left.

4. Open the Git bash.

5. Type the command "git clone" then paste the URL that you had copied in our 2nd step. The command should look as shown below:

   git clone https://github.com/YOUR-USERNAME/Cloned_Project_Name

6. Press the enter key and the local clone will be created.

After the cloning process is completed, you will have a copy of the project on your local computer.

Keeping the Fork in Sync

After forking a particular project in order to propose changes to original repository, it is possible for you to configure the git in order to pull the changes from original, or the upstream repository to your local clone of the fork. This can be done by following the steps given below:

1. Open the repository on GitHub.

2. Under the name of the repository, click "Clone or download".

3. In the section for Clone with HTTPs, click the icon with arrow pointing to the left in order to copy the

clone URL for the repository.

4. Open the Git Bash.

5. Change your directory to the location of the fork that you cloned in the 2nd step. To change your directory to your home directory, you only have to type the "cd" command with no other text. To see all the files and folders located in your current directory, just use the "ls" command. If you need to change directory to any of the listed directories, type "cd directory_name". To go up by one directory, just type the command "cd ..".

6. Type the command "git remote –v" then press the enter key. The currently configured remote repository r the fork will be shown:

git remote –v

7. Type the command "git remote add upstream" followed by the URL that you copied in the 2nd step

above then hit the enter key. The command should resemble the following:

git remote add upstream

https://github.com/nicohsam/SpoonKnife.git

However, the URL part should not be exactly as the one shown above.

8. If you need to verify the new upstream repository that you have specified for the fork, just re-run the "git remote –v" command. The URL for the fork will be shown as "origin", while the URL for original repository will be shown as "upstream".

You are now able to keep the fork synced with upstream repository using only a few Git commands.

Making Changes

On GitHub, you are able to change files, correct spelling mistakes, and add jokes to their homepage as well as any other details that you find. However, you must have noticed that this is yet to be collaboration. This is because the original repository will not be affected even after you begin to make the changes. There is a lot that you should do in order to contribute to your partner's project.

Accepting a Pull Request

As discussed earlier, a pull request is simple a way through which you can notify someone that you have made some changes which they should add to their repository. If one accepts your pull request, then the changes that you have made will be merged into their repository and they will be marked to have been done by you. Ensure that you describe your changes very well and ask the owner of the repository to add them to their repository.

If you receive a pull request from another GitHub, you will be notified. Review the changes that have been made and read the comments from the user.

After that, just add the changes to your repository so that they can be merged with your main project.

Chapter 5- Hosting Static Websites

With GitHub pages, you can directly host your website from your GitHub repository. After that, your site will be hosted in your own GitHub subdomain.

Automatic Page Generator

On GitHub, you are provided with an automated system that can bootstrap an empty repository for the GitHub pages. It allows you to pick from premade templates so that you will not have to clone the repository to your local machine.

Begin by creating a blank repository and give it any name that you want. Next, open the "Settings" tab. The generator will build only the front page for you. However, it is possible for you to get a lot done. The styles will be modern and new. You will be able to look at your site online. Since this is the first time, you may be required to wait for some time. After the first time, it will be quicker for you to publish.

Manual Creation

It is possible for you to create GitHub Pages site from a blank repository. However, you have to do some extra work by getting your HTML/CSS/JS code yourself then commit it to the repository.

The site will be on a branch named "gh-pages". In case you commit to master branch, which forms the default branch in git, GitHub will not care. It will check to see whether you have the "gh-pages" branch.

Begin by creating a new repository on GitHub then clone it locally. Ensure that you use your own command when running the clone command:

git clone git@github.com:nicohsam/blank.git

You will t6hen have cloned a blank repository and git will notify you about it. It has no initial commit or even a commit. Let us create a "gh-pages" branch for our initial files:

git checkout -b gh-pages

Then check the status of the repository:

git status

You will find that the branch has been created successfully. You can then get a minimal website.
Put the files for the website in your repository, add then commit them. This can be done by running the following commands:

git add index.html site.css site.js
git commit **-m "A Basic GitHub Pages site"**

After running the above commands, you will be ready to push to GitHub. However, it will be good for you to remember that we are pushing the "gh-pages", which currently does not exist on the GitHub repository. The push command should be as follows:

git push origin gh-pages

After pressing the enter key, you will be able to see the progress of the push command. Once the command completes, you will find the site has been published in the following URL:

http://username.github.com/repository-name

Chapter 6- Making Code Citable

DOI (Digital Object Identifiers) act as the backbone for metrics system and academic reference. It is possible for you to make your GitHub work citable by archiving the GitHub repository and assigning a DOI to it. This is of importance to researchers who need to cite their GitHub repositories in academic literature. This is what we will be discussing in this chapter and we will do it using the Zenodo data archiving tool.

For you to create a DOI, you should first choose the repository that you need to archive in Zenodo. To do this, open your repository then click the tab for "Repositories".

Next, you should login to Zenodo. Just open **Zenodo** and click Login button which you can find on the top right corner of the page. You will find that you are given an option to login with GitHub account.

The Zenodo will redirect you back to GitHub so that it may be authorized to share your email address and configure web hooks on the repositories. Permit it by clicking "Permit application" and it will get the permission that it needs.

Note that for you to archive a repository that belongs to an organization on GitHub, it will be good for you to ensure that the administrator for the organization has granted third-party access to Zenodo application.

You will have authorized the Zenodo application to configure repository web hooks that are needed to allow DOI-issuing and archiving. For you to enable this, just toggle the "On" button that is located next to your repository. Note that the Zenodo application is only capable of accessing public repositories, so make sure that the repository that you need to archive is public.

Checking Repository Settings

Once you enable archiving in Zenodo, you will have to setup some new web hook on the repository. On your repository, click the tab for "Settings", then move to the left hand menu and click "Web hooks". You will see that there is a new web hook that has been configured to send messages to the Zenodo application.

Creating a New Release

The default setting is that Zenodo will take an archive of the GitHub repository every time that you create a new release. To test it, just go to the main view of the repository and click on "releases" header item. If you had not created releases for the repository before, you will be prompted to "Create a new release". Click the button, and then fill in the details in the form that is provided. If it is the first release for the code, you should give it a version number of v1.0.0. Add in any notes for the release then click the button written "Publish release".

Once a new release has been created, it will trigger the Zenodo application to archive your repository. To confirm whether the process has taken place, click the "Upload" tab of the Zenodo application in your Zenodo profile. A new upload will be shown in the panel located on the right hand side.

Minting a DOI

Before the Zenodo application can assign a DOI to your repository, you should provide some details regarding the GitHub repository that you have archived. Check all the information regarding the description of your software and once you are happy, just clicks the "Publish" button which can be found at the bottom of Zenodo form. Congratulations, you will have made a DOI for the GitHub repository.

On the Zenodo GitHub page, you will see the repository listed alongside a shiny new badge that shows your new DOI.

Chapter 7- Managing Repository Collaborators

Several GitHub users can collaborate and work on a project running on a single repository. Let us discuss how this can be done.

Inviting Collaborators to a Repository

It is possible for you to invite collaborators to your personal repository. For the case of repositories that are owned by organizations, a more granular access can be granted to the users. Follow the steps given below:

1. Ask for the username of the individual you need to add as a collaborator. If they don't have, then ask them to sign up for an account on GitHub.

2. On GitHub, move to the main page of the repository.

3. Under the name of your repository, click "Settings".

4. Click "Collaborators" which is located on the left sidebar.

5. Begin to type the name of the collaborator under "Collaborators".

6. The collaborator's name will appear on the drop down, so choose it.

7. Next, click "Add Collaborator".

8. The user will then receive an invitation via their email address asking them to join the repository.

Removing a Collaborator from a Repository

Once you have removed a collaborator from your repository, they will no longer have a read/write access on it.

If it is a private repository and the user had created a fork of the repo, the fork will as well be deleted.

After the removal of a collaborator, the forks created from private repositories are deleted. However, clones of the repository will remain on the user's computer.

To remove a collaborator from a repository, follow the steps given below:

1. Open the main page of your GitHub repository.

2. Under the name of your repository, click "Settings".

3. Click "Collaborators & teams" on the left sidebar.

4. Identify the collaborator you need to remove from the repository, and then click the X icon next to his name.

Removing yourself from a Repository

Sometimes, you may no longer want to be part of someone else's repository. In such a case, you can opt to remove yourself, which is possible. To do this, follow the steps given below:

1. Open any page and click your profile photo which you can find on the upper right corner of the page. Next, click "Settings".

2. Click "Repositories" which you can find on the left sidebar.

3. Identify the repository that you want to leave then click the "Leave" button located next to it.

4. Read the warning keenly then click the option for "I understand, leave this repository".

Limiting Interaction with a Repository

It is possible for you to temporarily restrict how particular users comment, open issues or create pull requests in your public repository. Any user with admin or owner access to a particular repository is capable of restricting all the other users from interacting with the repository for a period of 24 hours. After the expiry of 24 hours, the regular permissions of the user will be restored. It is also possible for you to temporarily disable interactions from all the users whose accounts have been created in the last 24 hours, or from the users who are not prior collaborators or contributors for the repository. Follow the steps given below:

1. Navigate to the main page of the GitHub repository.

2. Under the name of the repository, click "Settings".

3. Select one or even more categories of the users under "Temporary interaction limits".

- If you need to limit the access to users whose accounts are more than 24 hours old, just choose "Limit to existing users".

- If you need to limit the access to the users who have previously made a commit to the master branch of the repository, choose the "Limit to prior contributors".

- To limit the access to the individuals who have a push access to the repository, choose "Limit to repository collaborators".

Reporting Spam or Abuse

Sometimes, you may spot an abuse or spam. This is any behavior that violates the terms and conditions of the GitHub repository. You should report such to the GitHub administrators by following the steps given below:

1. Visit the profile page of the user.

2. Under the profile picture of the user on the left sidebar, click "Block or report user".

3. Click "Report abuse".

4. A form will be presented to you. Complete the form by explaining to the GitHub support team the behavior of the user, then click "Send request".

Creating Team Discussions

Any member of an organization can create a public team discussion post. For you to be able to create a private team discussion post, it is a must for you to be the organization owner or a team member. The private posts will only be visible to the team members and the organization owners. For the case of public posts, they will be available to all members of the organization.

The following steps will help you create a team discussion:

1. Click your profile photo on the upper right corner of GitHub, and then click your "Your Profile".

2. Move to the left side of this page, then under "Organizations", click the organization icon.

3. Under the name of the organization, click "Teams".

4. On the tab for Teams, click the team name.

5. At the top of the page for the team, click "Discussions".

6. Type a title for the team discussion then add a comment in order to start the conversation.

7. Use the drop down menu to choose whether you need your post to be either private or public, but this is optional.

8. Click "Comment".

Conclusion

This marks the end of this book. Git is a tool for version control. When working on a project, the files will be of different versions depending on the time that you update them. These files can be tracked using the Git tool. The tool is used via a command line. GitHub provides you with a platform and a graphical user interface for project management. It is a good platform for you to collaborate with other users and work together on a particular project.